SC1

Dancers on the Beach
THE STORY OF THE GRUNION

Dancers on the Beach
THE STORY OF THE GRUNION

by Edward R. Ricciuti
illustrated by RICHARD CUFFARI

THOMAS Y. CROWELL COMPANY   New York

Acknowledgments

Many people helped with the research for this book. I am especially
grateful to Dr. George Ruggieri of the Osborn Laboratories of Marine
Sciences, New York Zoological Society, and to John Olguin, Cabrillo
Beach Marine Museum, City of Los Angeles.

ISBN 0-690-23158-X
1 2 3 4 5 6 7 8 9 10

Library of Congress Cataloging in Publication Data
Ricciuti, Edward R.
    Dancers on the Beach.
    SUMMARY: Discusses the physical characteristics and the mating and spawn-
ing process of the grunion, the only fish to lay its eggs on land.
    Bibliography: p. 49
    1. Grunion—Juv. lit. [1. Grunion. 2. Fishes] I. Cuffari, Richard, illus. II.
Title.
QL638.A8R47 1973   597'.58   73-3232
ISBN 0-690-23158-X

To *Ross Franco Nigrelli,* teacher and scientist, who seeks knowledge and shares it with equal fervor.

Contents

The Water Planet

Towards the edge of our galaxy, the Milky Way, a small planet orbits a rather ordinary star. The planet, however, is quite extraordinary, at least when compared with the eight other planets that share its star. Unlike any of its neighbors in space, this planet has an ocean. In it lives most of the planet's animal and plant life. Under its waves lies most of the planet's surface, with high mountains, deep valleys, and wide plains. Here and there, however, chunks of dry land rise above the ocean. Some of these dry land areas are large, but altogether they make up less than a third of the planet's surface. Seen from space, the planet seems a world of water. In fact, if visitors from elsewhere in the universe ever chance upon this little world, they probably will call it the Water Planet. We know it by another name: Earth.

Although people have named many different seas and oceans, the earth actually has only one great "world ocean." Its arms reach from one end of the globe to the other, encircling the continents. We humans think of ourselves as land creatures since no one lives permanently in the ocean. In one sense, however, we are children of the sea. Life on the earth began in the sea long before it spread to land. Today, in our salty body fluids, we carry a little bit of the ancient ocean within ourselves. The salts in human blood are in about the same proportion as in seawater, a reminder of where life came from.

The sea, swept by wind and wave and moving to the tides, seems to throb with life that goes on in almost numberless ways. Animals of just about every size, shape, and behavior live in the sea wherever they find a suitable place. Every animal, of sea or land, has a *habitat,* or place to live, that suits it best and a way of life that enables it to survive there. The role an animal plays in relation to the environment in which it lives is its *niche,* or place in the scheme of nature.

The sea, like the land, has many different zones inhabited by living things. The open sea is a vast pastureland, where float billions of tiny plants and

2

animals. Some are so small they cannot be seen with the unaided eye. Yet sometimes these tiny organisms multiply so rapidly they turn the water syrupy with their numbers. The floating organisms supply food for all sorts of larger creatures, from animals not much bigger than they, to the largest animal that ever lived, the blue whale.

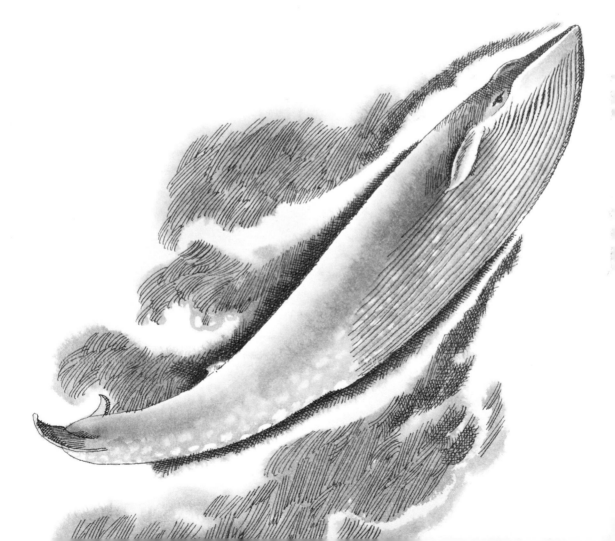

Deep in the ocean is another zone of life. The creatures that inhabit it can withstand the great pressure caused by the miles of water piled up above them. The giant squid, fifty feet long, roams the depths. So do even more fantastic creatures—like the viperfish, which carries its own lights, and the swallower fish *(Chiasmodus niger),* which can gulp down fish of its own size.

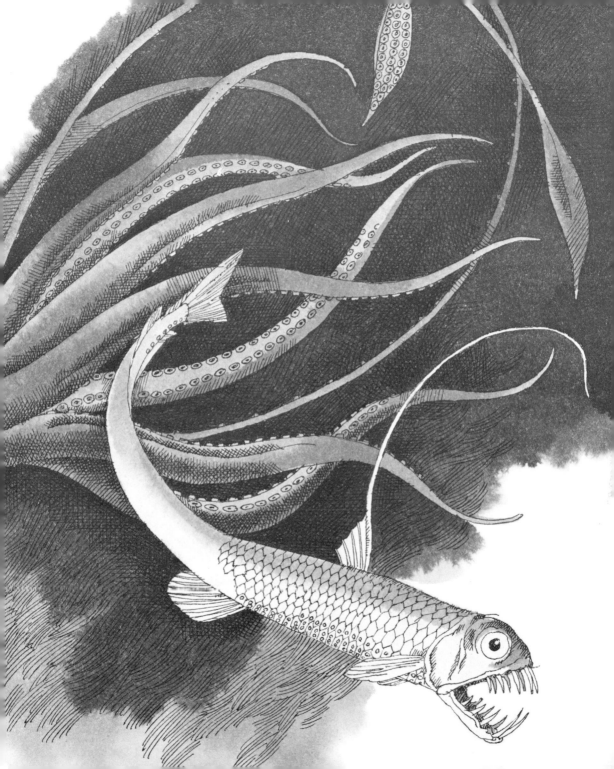

Unlike the other regions of the ocean, the tidal zone, where sea meets land, undergoes continual change. It is a difficult place to live, and the animals that make it their home have developed very special styles of life. Certain kinds of barnacles cling to rocks that are washed only by the waves of the highest tides for a few hours monthly. Yet they manage to squeeze into these few hours all the functions they need to continue living. Some animals spend their entire lives in the tidal zone. Others spend part of their lives there, and others begin life there amidst the crash of breakers and surf. Among these last is a very unusual little fish called the grunion.

Of all the thousands of fish that live in the ocean, only the grunion lays its eggs on the land. The adult grunion—slim, graceful, silvery creatures about six inches long—mate and leave fertilized eggs in the sand of the beach at places reached by the tide only a few times monthly. The egg laying, or spawning, of the grunion is so timed that while the young develop in the eggs they are high on the beach. By the time the young are ready to hatch, however, the tide again is reaching for the spot where they are buried. Scientists still do not understand exactly how the grunion reproduces according to such a marvelous time clock— geared to the changing tidal zone.

The scientific name of the grunion is *Leuresthes*

tenuis. It belongs to a family of fishes called the silversides, which includes 150 different kinds of fishes. Most of these small, shiny fishes live in salt water. Fishermen on the east coast of the United States use the Atlantic silversides as bait. In the Caribbean Sea, a silversides commonly seen swimming in large schools is the reef silversides. The grunion looks like most other silversides. It is a streamlined fish, from five inches to eight inches long. Grunion inhabit the waters off southern California and nearby Baja California in Mexico. They are most common between Point Conception, California, and Punta Abreojos, Mexico. Another kind of grunion (*Leuresthes sardina*) lives in the Gulf of California.

Most of the time grunion probably keep close to the surface of the sea. They often are seen amidst the floating beds of kelp that dot the waters off California. Few grunion are found more than a mile offshore, and scientists believe they spend their lives near the coastline, usually in from fifteen to forty feet of water.

Like people, fish are animals with a backbone. In fact, fish were the first animals to have a backbone. They swam in the ancient sea 400 million years ago, which was 100 million years before any other backboned animal lived on the earth. Of all the backboned animals, or vertebrates, that live in the water, fish remain best suited for life there—far better even than whales and dolphins.

Although the forms of fish vary, they are basically streamlined, more or less like a torpedo in shape. In fish that are flat, such as rays and flounders, the torpedo has been flattened. The fish's form is important because it takes less effort to move a streamlined object through water, which is eight hundred times denser than air.

The fish's form, together with the muscles in its body, enables it to wedge itself through the water. The fish actually pushes the water aside as it travels. When a fish swims, muscles from head to tail flex and relax in series. This sends a wave passing through the body to the tail, which moves from side to side and shoves

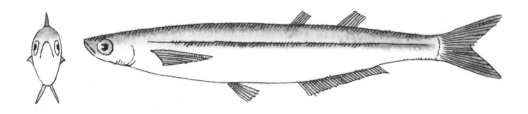

the fish ahead. If you could look at a fish swimming in slow motion, it would seem to wiggle in almost snake-like fashion. The fish's fins help to propel it, and also serve as rudders.

Of course, the key to the fish's success in the water is not its shape but its ability to breathe there. The organs that enable a fish to do so are its gills, folded flaps of delicate tissue in the head. The gills contain a great number of very fine blood vessels, close to the surface. When a fish breathes, water enters through the mouth, passes over the gills, and is forced out through openings in the side of the fish's head. As the water moves over the gills, a vital exchange takes place. Oxygen dissolved in the water enters the fish's bloodstream, and carbon dioxide, a waste product in the blood, is carried away by the water.

How does this trade of waste carbon dioxide for life-giving oxygen work? The secret lies in the blood vessels. The walls of the vessels are very thin, and oxygen and carbon dioxide, both gases, can pass across them. Much the same process occurs when *you* breathe. The insides of your lungs are lined with very small blood vessels. Oxygen in the air that you inhale is carried to the lungs, where it comes in contact with the vessels. The difference between your way of breathing and that of most fish is that you get oxygen from the air and they get it from the water.

Some fish can breathe air, however, as well as water. The climbing perch of Asia, for example, has organs that enable it do do so, and it sometimes travels overland from pond to pond. If one pond dries up it can move to another, and survive a drought. Scientists say that the climbing perch has become adapted to living as and where it does; in other words, it fits into its special niche. The organs that help the perch breathe air are called an *adaptation.* All living creatures have adaptations that suit them to a particular way of life in a particular environment, and these adaptations are the results of long-term adjustments in body and behavior.

The environment in which an animal lives is always changing, in ways large and small. Wind and water wear away mountains. Forests replace marshes. Sand

10

swirls across deserts where ocean waves once tossed. Most of these changes take great periods of time, often millions of years. Today, however, man is changing the environment almost overnight, by turning forests to wasteland, polluting the air and water, and turning valleys into artificial lakes.

If an animal cannot change with its environment, it will disappear, as its niche no longer fits into the scheme of nature. Those species of animals that exist on the earth today have been able to adapt to changing conditions, so far. It may take thousands of years for a species to change, or adapt, but it must do so or vanish.

Adaptation has enabled fish to occupy a fantastic assortment of niches. It has created tremendous variety in the 20,000 species of living fish—in the ways they appear, behave, and live out their life cycles.

You can tell much about the conditions under which a fish lives from looking at it. The stonefish, which lives on reefs of the Indian Ocean, is the most venomous fish in the world. Many barefooted fishermen have been killed by stepping on the stonefish, whose venom is delivered through spines on its back. The stonefish is a chunky, squat creature covered with lumps, warts, and other growths. It looks for all the world like a hunk of battered stone or coral, and is perfectly camouflaged when lying on the reef. It hardly moves,

Stonefish

until a smaller fish comes near. Then, with dazzling speed, it snaps up the smaller fish in its bulldog jaws.

The mackerel, unlike the stonefish, is a creature of the open water. It is very streamlined in shape and a fast swimmer. Its upper body is marked with blue-green bars, which form a pattern much like sunlight filtering the waves, and so it is very difficult to see from a boat.

The anglerfish, which lives in the depths where sunlight never reaches, has evolved organs that produce light. This adaptation also helps the anglerfish reproduce, for it is by its living lanterns that this creature attracts a mate.

Anglerfish

Adaptation is a natural process that cannot be directed by the animal which experiences it. Take the case of the mackerel, for instance. Ages ago, perhaps, an ancestor of the mackerel was hatched that was slightly different from the other young. Possibly it had a more streamlined body than its brothers and sisters, so that it swam faster and was more successful at catching prey and at escaping larger fish that hunted it. Therefore it survived and passed its traits on to its young, which also had superior streamlining and superior swimming ability. These fish, and then their young, survived in greater numbers than did the mackerel without their advantages, until eventually

13

all mackerel shared their characteristics. This is, of course, a simplified version, for many factors in an animal's environment influence adaptation.

The adaptations that shape grunion to begin life in the tidal zone apparently help their species to survive. In some way the grunion can sense forces that stem from the far-off moon and sun and create the rhythm of the earth's tides. The story of the grunion is one of surf boiling up a beach, of moonlight glistening on small dancers on the sand, and of tiny young fish buried beneath the feet of unsuspecting bathers. It is a story that can make us wonder how much we yet have to learn about the mysteries of life.

Dancers on the Beach

Three days have passed since the new moon. Tonight only a thin crescent is visible, 240,000 miles away in cold, black space. From the sandy beach the ocean looks as inky as the sky, and they blend at the horizon. Far from shore the lights of a lone ship seem to hang in black nothingness. It is difficult even to see the waves; the surf seems to rear up suddenly as it booms foaming on the sand. As each wave hits, its wash swirls up to the night's high-tide mark and then slides back into the dark sea.

The high-tide mark tonight is not as high up on the beach as on the night of the new moon. Tonight's tide peaked and turned ten minutes ago. There is no sound but the crash of surf, no light but that from the distant stars and the sliver of moon hanging in the sky.

Offshore, thirty or forty feet from where the breakers roll up on the beach, the small, silvery dancers have been gathering. Every few moments a slim form flashes near the surface of the sea. A grunion run is about to begin.

Another wave surges up the beach in a rush of foam. Silver gleams in the bubbles. As the wave retreats, a grunion appears suddenly out of the foam. The sides of the fish are silvery, its back blue-green. For a moment the grunion lies still on the smooth, wet sand. Then it flops from side to side, catches the wash of the next wave that sweeps over it, and rides back to the sea.

Several more waves break on the beach and then retreat. Another grunion appears, stranded on the sand. It glitters in the moonlight as it, too, returns to the sea on the next wave. Now other waves are stranding fish here and there along the beach. Twenty minutes have passed since the first fish appeared, and the run is about to begin in earnest.

As the foam from a large wave subsides, it reveals not one or two grunion but a whole clump of silvery forms. This time the fish do not return to the sea. Fins spread, they swim against the wash, struggling to stay on the beach. All along the waterfront other knots of fish emerge from the waves. In the dark of night on the shore of southern California, the dance of the grunion has begun.

The grunion on the beach seem to have a definite purpose. A close look at one of them shows it is making a tremendous effort to move up the beach. This one is a female ready to lay her eggs. She swims against the backwash of the waves, wriggling on the wet sand. Then, at a point just above the highest reach of the waves, she raises her head, arches her body, and drills into the sand with her tail. As she moves her tail back and forth, her body sinks deeper into the loose sand. Soon she is buried up to her pectoral fins, which spread and anchor her in place.

Meanwhile the male grunion have been working their way toward the female. From one to eight males may mate with a single female. Leaving wriggly trails in the wet sand, they surround the half-buried female. Each male tries to wrap around the female, with his underside toward her. As the males crowd around the female they discharge milt, which trickles into the hole dug by the female's tail. At the bottom of the hole, meanwhile, the female has deposited an orange egg cluster or pod about the size of a large olive. It contains more than a thousand eggs, which are fertilized when the milt seeps down to them.

Less than a minute has passed since the female beached herself. Now her task on the beach is finished and she struggles to free herself from the damp sand. The males already are catching waves that carry them back to the sea. The female wriggles out of the hole she has dug, then rests quietly for a moment. She moves again, this time to raise her small head. Her mouth opens and closes, and anyone close enough to hear can make out a tiny sound coming from the tired fish. To some people the noise sounds like a squeak. Others think it resembles a grunt; and this seems to be how the grunion got its name—from the word *gruñón,* Spanish for "one who grunts."

As the leading edge of a large wave reaches up to the female, she stirs, then vanishes in the bubbling water.

Grunion can live as long as twenty minutes on the beach, but most leave right after spawning. Within a few moments after the female returns to the water the hole where she buried her eggs is filled with glistening wet sand.

Elsewhere, all along the beach, the run continues. Hundreds, maybe thousands, of other grunion are coming ashore. When the run reaches its height, about an hour after it began, the beach is carpeted with squirming, silvery grunion. In the moments between the breaking of the waves you can hear the soft sounds of thousands of fish bodies flopping on the wet sand.

As time passes the waves bring in fewer and fewer

fish. By the time the tide has dropped about a foot from its high point of the night, no grunion remain on the beach. The spawning run, which lasted three hours, is over. Under the surface of the sand, however, uncounted thousands of fertilized orange grunion eggs are buried.

Each fertilized egg is about one-sixteenth of an inch in diameter, pinhead size. After the run is over the action of the waves and tides casts more and more sand over the egg clusters until they are six inches below the surface.

Meanwhile, a young grunion has started to develop within the thin covering, or membrane, that encloses each fertilized egg. Within four days a tiny gray fish has formed within the clear membrane. The thread-like body of the young fish is coiled tightly around the yolk that nourishes it. Its round eyes seem huge when compared to its tiny body.

Soon the little grunion begins to move its tail, and its small heart can be seen beating. Before six days have passed the blood pumped by the heart is visible, and at the age of a week the little grunion really begins to look like a fish. The yolk sac has shrunk to almost nothing by the eighth day, and now the little fish moves continually. Its eyes, which seem to have grown even bigger, are shiny circles with dark black centers. The young grunion is ready to hatch on the

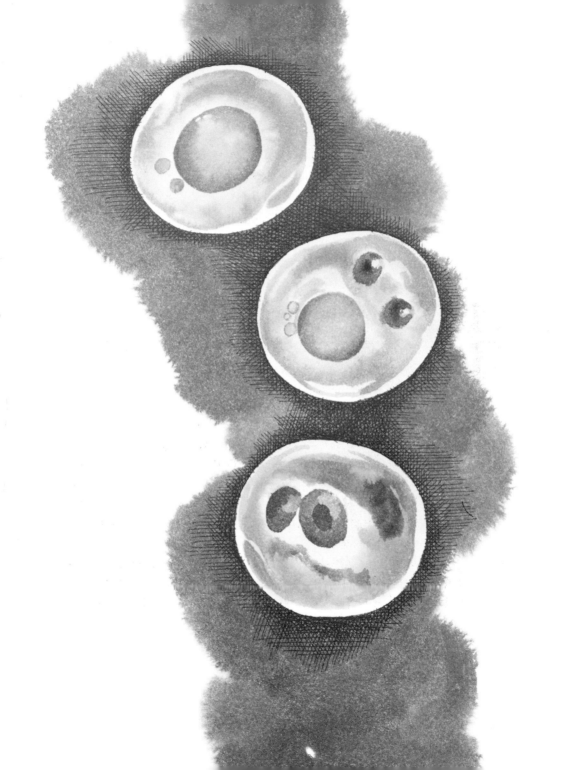

ninth day. But until the tide is high enough to reach the place where the grunion and its fellows are buried in the sand, they will not hatch.

The grunion's spawning season begins late in February or in early March. It is in full swing by mid-April, and ends by late August or September. Older grunion spawn first, while grunion hatched the year before are not ready to spawn until April or May. The grunion runs are heaviest, therefore, during April, May, and June, when all grunion, older fish and yearlings, are spawning. Young females lay about 1,000 eggs at each spawning, while older ones can produce three times that number on one run. This means that during the season an older female, spawning up to eight times, can lay 24,000 eggs.

Grunion do not take care of their eggs or young, but by burying their eggs in the sand they help them survive. There are as many different ways in the animal kingdom of having young and providing for them as there are animals. From grunion to elephant the patterns differ, yet the object is the same— survival. If a species is to continue to exist, enough of its young must reach adulthood to reproduce yet another generation.

Animals that produce vast numbers of young often make no provisions for their offspring. The ocean sunfish, which can weigh more than 1,000 pounds,

Sunfish

can produce 28 million eggs in a single season, but takes no care of them. A codfish can loose up to 9 million eggs in the sea during breeding. Probably the cod never sees her eggs again. At any rate, they float freely at the mercy of wind, wave, and current. They can be washed up on the shore, or into polluted waters. Sea birds can scoop them up and fish can feed on them. But with so many eggs produced by female codfish, chances are very good that enough eggs will survive to produce a new generation. So far this pattern has worked for the cod.

Animals that have smaller numbers of young, on the

other hand, generally provide for them in some way. Maybe the special provision is a nest where the young hatch unguarded. Or maybe the parents feed and guard the young. In any case, some kind of help from the parents gives the young an advantage in the struggle to survive.

The female bluegill sunfish lays from 3,000 to 19,000 eggs—not many for a fish of its size. The male bluegill builds a nest of pebbles for the female's eggs. After she leaves the eggs in the nest, the male guards it, and fans fresh water over it with his fins. He even will attack much larger fish that come near the nest.

The female Pacific salmon, which lays only about 800 eggs, builds a nest herself. With her fins she fans away the pebbles and gravel on the bottom of a stream, making a saucer-shaped hole. The eggs are round, like pebbles, and are heavy and sticky enough to stay on the bottom while the female covers them with gravel.

Giving the young a head start in life can use up much of the parent's energy. The male bluegill must be on the alert at all times, rushing back and forth to chase away enemies. The salmon, after spawning, rests near the bottom, exhausted; after a while it dies. It is a life-and-death struggle for the spawning grunion to hide their eggs on the beach and to get back into the ocean.

24

Time, Tides, and Grunion

The spawning runs of the grunion occur at exactly the right time so that the fertilized eggs will not be disturbed by the tide until they are ready to hatch. If this does not seem so remarkable, think for a moment about the forces that cause the tides.

Most parts of the ocean experience two high tides and two low tides daily. The tides are caused by many complicated forces stemming from the movement of the earth, the moon, and, to a lesser degree, the sun. The main cause of the tides is the pull of the moon and the sun on the earth. The moon, however, is the real mother of the tides, for it is so much nearer the earth that the effect of its pull is almost triple that of the sun. The pull of the moon and sun tugs at the waters of the ocean nearest to them, causing a bulge in the ocean. The nearest waters, and actually the entire half of the earth nearest the moon and sun, are pulled away from the waters on the opposite side of the globe, making another bulge there. The two bulges on opposite sides of the globe are the high tides. Midway between them are the low tides.

As the earth spins in an easterly direction on its axis, the high-tide bulges travel westward across the face of the globe. In the course of a day both bulges pass over many parts of the earth, causing two high tides and two low tides daily. However, tides at places very near one another may be quite different, for they are also affected by conditions in the atmosphere, the depth of the sea, the shape of the shoreline, and many other things.

Twice monthly, extra-high tides—called spring tides—occur. This happens at new moon and full moon, when the earth, moon, and sun are directly in line and the moon and sun pull in the same direction. New moon and full moon are fourteen days apart. After a spring tide the place reached by the high tide retreats down the beach, dropping each day. A low point between the spring tides is reached in a week, and then once more the high-tide mark edges up the beach, day by day, until the next spring tide occurs.

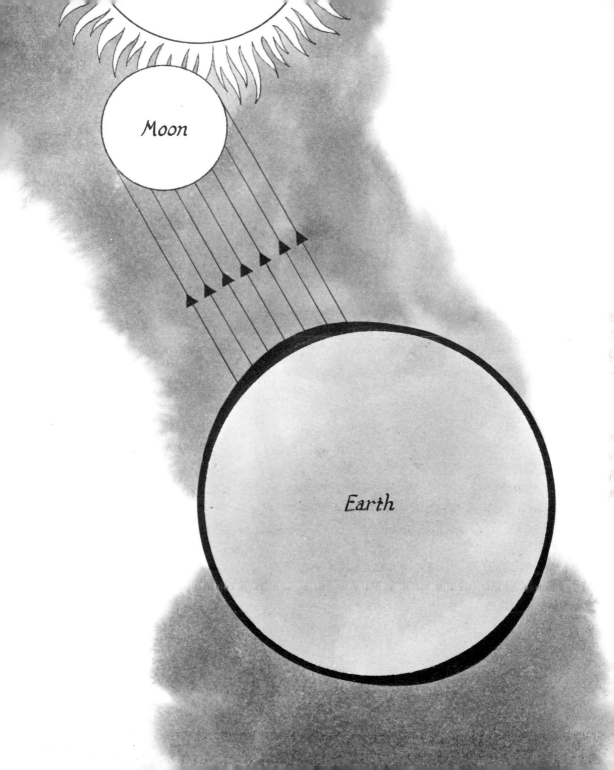

Many kinds of animals have a sense of timing that attunes them to the daily rise and fall of the tides, and some are attuned to the cycle covering the period from one spring tide to another. Animals, in fact, can sense a wide variety of rhythmic changes in their surroundings. In nature an animal's surroundings change regularly, from night to day, season to season. Daylight lengthens as summer approaches and decreases as winter nears. To survive, animals must adjust their body processes and behavior so that they are in harmony with these cycles in nature. The inner sense of timing that enables animals to do so is not fully understood by scientists. For want of a better name, however, it is called a biological clock.

Some experiments make it seem as if regular outside conditions such as changes in light trigger biological clocks within some animals. Other experiments, however, indicate that certain biological clocks operate even when animals are removed from their normal surroundings. No matter how they operate, biological clocks are important adaptations. They regulate an animal's life in ways that help it survive.

Biological clocks seem to time a wide variety of natural cycles. Some are set on a daily cycle. The fact that most people grow tired in the evening and wake in the morning is believed to be a demonstration of this kind of biological clock. Other clocks work on a monthly or yearly basis. Many animals, including the grunion, are ready to breed during only one part of the year. This readiness results from changes in their bodies timed by biological clocks. The clock of the grunion seems to work according to three rhythms: the lunar cycle—(new moon, first quarter, full moon, last quarter); the daily rise and fall of the tides; and the annual cycle that determines the breeding season.

Some of the most curious biological clocks are regulated by the lunar cycle and the daily rise and fall of the tides. The fiddler crab, which lives in colonies on seaside mud flats, has a clock that lets it know when the tide is changing. Fiddlers live in burrows in the mud and feed on small animals and bits of organic matter they find on the beach at low tide. During high tide the fiddlers stay in their burrows, not feeding. But when the tide changes and begins to drop, the fiddlers start coming out of their burrows to hunt food. By the time the tide is high once again, the crabs have retreated into their burrows.

Perhaps the most spectacular biological clocks, however, are those that time the reproduction of animals. In burrows tunneled through the dead coral of South Pacific reefs lives a worm whose breeding cycle is adjusted to the phases of the moon. This little animal, the palolo worm, does not like light. It feeds outside of its burrow only when the night is darkest. The palolo worm shuns even moonlight, except when it is time to breed. Palolo worms breed during the first night of the last quarter of the moon in October and November. At these times the worms creep from their burrows and swarm toward the surface of the sea. Thousands gather until the water is thick with them. The people of the nearby islands gather, too, for the

Whitefish

worms are considered a delicacy. As the dawn breaks the worms spawn, loosing their eggs in the sea. When spawning is over they swim back to their burrows, and by full daylight they have vanished from the surface of the sea.

Some biological clocks regulate the breeding of animals so that their young will appear at the time when conditions are best for them. In the cold waters of the Great Lakes, schools of whitefish spawn near shore during the winter. The young fish develop in the eggs for up to five months before they hatch. This means that they will not hatch until the winter has passed, and the water, warmed, is filled with food. Black bass, on the other hand, spawn in spring and summer, but

their eggs hatch in just a few days. In both instances the young fish hatch when conditions favor survival and growth.

Adult grunion spawn only after the highest tides of the fourteen-day lunar cycle have peaked, when the tides that follow will be lower than those of the night before. If the young are to hatch they must have nine or ten days to develop before the water reaches them. Usually the adults spawn on the three or four nights following the spring tide, which gives the young enough time.

The exact timing by which the adult grunion spawn is truly marvelous. If, for instance, they spawned when the lunar tidal cycle was rising instead of dropping, the young would be washed out before they were ready to hatch. The same disaster would happen to the young if the eggs were laid before the night's high tide had peaked.

Why do the grunion spawn only at night? During the spawning season the beaches of southern California experience two high tides daily, one always lower than the other. It just happens that the highest of the two tides is the one that occurs at night. If the grunion were to spawn on the high tide during the day, the evening's high water would flood the newly fertilized eggs.

The grunion that live in the Gulf of California, on

the other hand, spawn in the daytime, because in the gulf the highest of the two daily high tides occurs during the day rather than at night.

Unless there are unusual storms that send waves high up on the beach, the rising water just before the next spring tide after the spawning will find the young grunion ready for life in the sea. Then, as the waves churn up the sand, the young grunion in their clear globes swirl about with sand grains in the water. Within a minute or two the covering that has protected each little fish splits, and the grunion's quarter-inch-long body uncoils like a spring, popping into the water. For a moment the little fish wriggles, as if stretching itself. Then almost immediately it begins to feed on tiny organisms, called plankton, in the water. Many

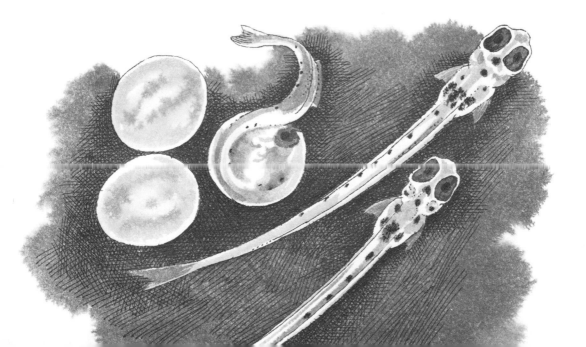

other fishes, unlike the grunion, cannot capture food immediately after hatching. The grunion's ability to do so is an adaptation that helps it survive in the surf. As the little grunion gobbles food, its stomach fills and forms a black dot in its nearly transparent body, which already is growing in size. At the same time the little fish is being swept out to sea. It all happens so quickly that in just a few minutes all the young grunion have hatched and have been swept from the beach to the safety of the sea.

What happens if for some reason the water does not reach the eggs? Young grunion can survive for a month in the damp sand of the beach. So, if they are not washed free during the tidal cycle in which they were spawned, they can live until the water reaches for them a second time. The adult grunion do not know that their eggs would perish if they spawned at the wrong time. They do not know that the way in which they reproduce their kind seems so remarkable. Nor did they choose it over other ways. It is a pattern inherited from the past, fixed in each grunion's being, and for grunion it is the only way.

Science and the Grunion

No one knows who was the first person to watch the grunion glittering on a beach at night. Perhaps it was a prehistoric hunter or fisherman. Did he understand that the grunion were spawning? At any rate, not until the early years of this century did scientists discover the fascinating secret of why the grunion stranded themselves on the beach. Scientists first observed the grunion in the 1860s. But the first major scientific study of this little fish occurred in 1919. It was carried on by Dr. Will (William) F. Thompson of the California State Fisheries Laboratory. Thompson stood in the surf during the dark of night, carefully observed what the grunion were doing, and recorded the true story behind their runs.

Dr. Thompson, who was only five feet four inches tall, was small in body but strong in will. He was a dedicated scientist and a hard worker who expected all who worked with him to share his dedication. By the time he died in 1965, he had earned worldwide fame for his knowledge of fish and the way they live.

When Dr. Thompson began his observations, few people outside of southern California had heard of the grunion. Many thought the tales of the grunion runs were fables. Some of the people who saw the runs suspected the grunion were laying eggs, but they understood little else. Others claimed the fish were trying to commit suicide, or fleeing from an enemy. The real meaning of the grunion run was explained by

Dr. Thompson in July 1919, when he published a
report, "The Spawning of the Grunion," in the *Bulletin* of the California Fish and Game Commission. The
run, Dr. Thompson claimed, was "one of the most
marvelous in the many strange chapters in the life
histories of fish," and "one of the really remarkable
stories in the annals of natural history."

Dr. Thompson, helped by his wife, Julia, started his
observations April 15, 1919. Under a full moon he
waited in the night on a broad sweep of sandy shore at
Long Beach, California. No grunion appeared. The
next night, however, Thompson found his grunion, as
he did on the two nights that followed.

During the spawning run the grunion seem to appear from nowhere out of the surf. It appears that a few grunion may test the beach, like scouts, ahead of the main run. They are males. For more than an hour before the run, the grunion cruise back and forth parallel to the beach, just offshore. Dr. Thompson discovered this by wading into the water shortly before he expected a run to occur. Using a seine, he netted masses of grunion.

Dr. Thompson then measured the grunion he had seined and found that the females generally were longer than the males. When he later observed grunion on the beach, he was therefore able to tell that only females buried themselves in the sand. Watching the males gather around the females, Dr. Thompson understood that the fish were mating. "The conclusion is irresistible," he said. The females deposited their eggs while the males fertilized them. Dr. Thompson timed how long it took for the eggs to be produced and fertilized, and he found that this often occurred in less than half a minute. He dug up some of the eggs and found that they were only an inch or two below the surface. When he looked over the surface of the sand with a searchlight, however, he found no eggs there.

During the day after the spawning run Dr. Thompson tested his observations of the night before. The eggs he had found were two inches deep at most. He

had measured the distance between the pectoral fins of the female and her vent, the opening where the eggs appear. It also measured two inches. But when Thompson dug up eggs the day after the run, he was surprised, for many of the eggs were five and six inches beneath the surface. To place eggs this deep, a female would have to bury herself to the tip of her snout. Dr. Thompson, however, had seen females buried only to their pectoral fins. Possibly, he reasoned, the females use their tails to push their eggs deeper into the sand. But if this was so, the sand would mix with the eggs, and he found no sand in the egg clusters. Just to make sure the pods he had dug up really were those of the grunion, he compared the eggs in the pods to those taken from female grunion. They matched. For a time, then, Dr. Thompson could not explain why the egg pods were covered by so much sand.

Meanwhile, however, he set out to study how the action of the tides and waves on the sand affected the spawning of the grunion. He had seen the fish spawn just below the point reached by the highest water of the night, as the tide retreated. At this point the sand of the beach was heavily stirred by the waves, which made it easier for the females to dig in their tails. Dr. Thompson drove low posts into the sand for several feet down the beach to find out what happened to the sand during the rise and fall of a single tide.

For two hours before high tide and two hours after it had peaked, he measured the depth of sand at the posts. Dr. Thompson discovered that the incoming waves pile up a lip of sand ahead of them. As the tide recedes the lip forms lower and lower on the beach. Here was the key to why the pods Dr. Thompson had found during the day were buried at a greater depth than those he observed the night before. After the grunion leave the beach the waves pile more and more sand over the pods. Thus the grunion's way of spawning is adapted not only to the rise and fall of the tide but to the action of the waves on the beach as well.

Dr. Thompson also experimented with young grunion to learn about the way they developed before hatching. Being buried in the sand of the beach would destroy the unhatched young of any other fish but the grunion. Dr. Thompson put unhatched grunion in fresh water, rather than seawater, and found that, even a week later, they still lived. He could see the heart of each little fish beating within the clear membrane that surrounded the tiny creature. The membrane, Dr. Thompson concluded, protects the unhatched grunion from fresh water that soaks the beach during heavy rains. After hatching, however, grunion die if placed in fresh water.

The membrane around the developing grunion also protects them from drying—if they are covered by sand. Dr. Thompson proved this by placing unhatched young on a blotter, which he used as a substitute for the surface of the sand. The young fish dried up within five hours, but others that had been placed in a covered dish survived. The cover of the dish, like the covering of sand over the developing grunion, helps conserve moisture the little fish needs to live.

Buried in the sand, the young also are hidden from enemies. Dr. Thompson observed, however, that a small beetle burrows into the pods and feeds on them. He found beetles in pods that he had uncovered, and watched a beetle eat the unhatched grunion when placed in a jar with them. Shore birds also eat the buried young, and on a beach near San Diego ground squirrels have been seen feeding on them. One squirrel examined by scientists had the remains of four-hundred fertilized grunion eggs in its stomach.

Dr. Thompson was fascinated by the way the little grunion escape from the sand. To find out exactly how they do it he kept daily watch over places where he knew the young were buried. Each day he dug them up to see if they remained, then reburied them exactly where he had found them. Eventually there came a tide high enough to sweep over the eggs, and they disappeared from the beach. Dr. Thompson then knew that it was the incoming tide which released the young grunion from their buried hiding places.

He still was uncertain, however, whether the fish hatched before or after they were uncovered. An accident helped him find out. To separate the fertilized eggs he needed for experiments from the sand in which they were buried, Dr. Thompson would shake the mixture in a container of seawater. One day while he was doing this the grunion hatched. The newly hatched grunion were from a batch of eggs laid during a run ten days earlier. Since the tide reached the place on the beach where they had been buried just about the time they hatched in Dr. Thompson's container, it was clear that the young grunion developed in time to hatch when the water was high enough to reach them.

Dr. Thompson next put unhatched young, still covered by sand, in a dish which he slowly flooded with seawater. But the fish did not hatch. The next day he uncovered the young fish and they hatched almost immediately, showing that the grunion hatch only after the waves wash them from the sand. To be doubly certain, Dr. Thompson repeated his experiment many times. Today scientists suspect that when the waves surge over the unhatched young, a chemical reaction causes the covering around each grunion to split.

Once a young grunion is in the sea, it starts growing quickly. It is five inches long and ready to spawn in a year. As spawning time approaches, the fish's bodily processes change, and it stops growing temporarily. Each year, when a grunion's growth stops, a scar forms on each scale of the fish. The scars can be seen under a microscope and are used to tell the age of grunion. As spawning time nears, the energy that was used for growth is directed to the fish's reproductive organs, which grow larger. In the female, the first batch of eggs ripens.

Grunion begin to grow again when the spawning season is over. They usually have a lifespan of two or three years, although some live a year longer. After the first year, however, they grow more slowly. Actually, since spawning occurs in spring and summer, grunion grow only in the fall and winter.

After Dr. Thompson reported what he had discovered about the grunion, other scientists began to wonder if grunion returned to spawn where they hatched, as some fish do. Eels, for instance, hatch far out to sea, hundreds of miles off Bermuda, and then begin to head toward Europe or North America. After traveling thousands of miles, which may take more than two years, the eels swim up rivers. They may stay in the rivers for a number of years, but when the time to spawn approaches they head back to mid-ocean to lay their eggs.

Experiments in 1928 by Dr. Frances N. Clark of the California State Fisheries Laboratory showed that the grunion do not necessarily spawn where they themselves hatched. (It was Dr. Clark who discovered that the female grunion may spawn all season long.) During 1927 a beach had been built south of Los Angeles. Because this area, Cabrillo Beach, was new, grunion never had spawned or hatched there. The beach had been built of sand pumped from the ocean bottom just offshore and spread on either side of a long rock breakwater. Frances Clark visited Cabrillo Beach on nights that followed the spring tide and found thousands of grunion hopping on the sand. From that time on grunion began to spawn on Cabrillo Beach.

Grunion runs are a special event in southern California. The grunion, which are very good to eat, may be scooped off the beach by hand. Grunion hunters are not allowed to use nets or traps. They dart and run after the silvery fish, often in the glow of bonfires built above the high-water mark. Catching and holding a slippery grunion is very difficult, and people often end up with empty hands while the fish squirm off to sea.

During the 1920s fishing for grunion with nets and pollution of the water caused a sharp drop in the number of these fish. California in 1926 set aside the months of April, May, and June as a closed season when no one could take grunion. This meant that the grunion could spawn two or three times before anyone tried to catch them. By 1947 there were again enough grunion to make it permissible to hunt them in June.

Over untold ages grunion have adapted successfully to a unique way of life. But if we continue to pollute our great "world ocean," neither the grunion nor many other fish will survive. Few fish can adapt to pollution. If people can learn to live with nature, on the other hand, it is likely that the grunion will continue to exist on the Water Planet.

Bibliography

BRIDGES, WILLIAM. *The New York Aquarium Book of the Water World.* New York: American Heritage Press, 1970.

ENGEL, LEONARD, and the Editors of *Life. The Sea.* New York: Time, Inc., 1961.

MARSHALL, NORMAN and OLGA. *Ocean Life.* New York: The Macmillan Company, 1971.

NORMAN, J. R., and GREENWOOD, P. H. *A History of Fishes.* New York: Hill & Wang, 1963.

THORSON, GUNNAR. *Life in the Sea.* New York: McGraw Hill Book Company, 1971

Index

51

About the Author

Edward R. Ricciuti was born in New York City and grew up in Connecticut, and he earned degrees from the University of Notre Dame and Columbia University. From 1967 to 1972 Mr. Ricciuti was curator of publications and public relations of the New York Zoological Society, where he edited *Animal Kingdom*, a popular bimonthly; *Zoologica*, a scientific quarterly; and other publications. He also wrote and directed films for the Society's five institutions, including the Bronx Zoo and New York Aquarium. A veteran of several scientific expeditions on land and sea and a certified scuba diver, Mr. Ricciuti now devotes full time to writing, lecturing, and television appearances. He is a member of the cast of "Patchwork Family," a WCBS-TV (New York) program for children. Mr. Ricciuti's books for children and adults reflect his deep interest in animal behavior and conservation. He now lives with his family in Killingworth, Connecticut.

About the Illustrator

Richard Cuffari's paintings have been exhibited in several New York galleries. A number of his illustrations have appeared in the design shows of the American Institute of Graphic Arts and in the annual exhibits of the Society of Illustrators.

A native of New York, Mr. Cuffari studied at Pratt Institute. He lives in Brooklyn with his wife and four children.